Praise for M....

"If you long to be a true influencer in this world, Chaz can show you how!"

— CORY HARTMAN, age 9

"I have watched Chaz build his own platform from the ground up to become the largest in the world. And he has done so by using the strategies and tips he outlines in this very practical book. And by platform I mean this wooden, elevated thing in his living room. Wait, you were talking about something else?"

— SHERRY MARRIOT, author's mother

"Chaz Marriot is a pioneer in social media who is now generously sharing his 'secrets' with those of us who have been marveling at his success for many years."

— LAURA INGALLS-WILDER, actual pioneer

"Chaz Marriot is a futuristic visionary who also still owes me, roughly, fifty-eight dollars. What he has here, is a book."

— TED KLUCK, award-winning author, entrepreneur

.

"Yes, talent, desire and passion are key elements for success as an author. But this book identifies the elephant in the room   that talent, desire and passion really don't mean a [expletive] thing."

— RENNY HARLAN, artist

"Chaz Marriot is a pig."

— RACHEL HELD-BOLTZ-EVANS-WEBER, feminist

"One word: Integrity. And I'll leave it up to you to interpret the meaning of that, vis' Chaz Marriot, one way or the other."

— RON NEPHEWS, leader

"Chaz Marriot is taller than average."

— JENNIFER COLIN, former classmate

"It's almost as if this book was less about useful business theory, and more just the memoir of a sad guy. If I could give it zero stars, I wood [SIC]."

—AMAZON CUSTOMER

"If you'd like to expand your platform, read *Mega* and then read it again. Your success depends on it. Chaz Marriot is the Sensei of business. He is the Sifu of social media. Chaz Marriot will never die . . . he will, like some Egyptian pharaohs, live on forever, bedecked in jewels and surrounded by female admirers who regularly fan him and feed him grapes, sexily. If you would like that (or some version thereof) to happen to you, you need to read this book."

— CHAZ MARRIOT

MEGA

GET NOTICED ALL THE TIME, FOR EVERYTHING

CHAZ MARRIOT

www.gutcheckpress.com

Lansing   Grand Ledge   New York*

Mega: Get Noticed All the Time, for Everything

The following is a work of satire, published without malice. Any similarity
to real persons, living or dead, is therefore just for yucks. Get over it.

ISBN 978-0-9830783-6-4
Published in association with K-D Enterprises and Cardiff Giant.

* By New York, we of course mean Altoona, Pennsylvania

"Change is the only constant."

–Chaz Marriot

"This Isn't Just a Conference Booth,
It's an Extension of My Body"

It's no accident that I'm starting my magnum opus on business from this conference booth. This isn't just a conference booth. I think of it as an extension of my personal brand and even, at times, an extension of my body.

You see, this stack of business cards and this bowl of free candy aren't merely tchotchkes for weary conferees. They are a conduit to my Twitter feed, my Facebook page, my YouTube account, my Instagram, my Tumblr, my Vine, and even my MySpace page—which are themselves conduits to my entire online persona. When a publisher, a band, or a stay-at-home mom writing frontier romances hires me to do their publicity, they don't just get a marketing and social media expert—they get all of me. My heart, my soul, my handsome-but-not-intimidating JC Penny's smile, and my extensive collection of conference golf shirts.

I am a self-contained unit.

My passions are synergy, creativity, enthusiasm, leadershifting, paradigm-shifting, and also passion. I also like those over-the-ear micro-phones that allow you to move around.

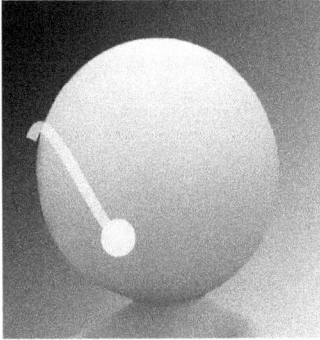

Here I am, wearing the kind of microphone thing I'm talking about. Some of the newer ones are even less noticeable!

If there's one thing I learned in my three-plus years of owning a legitimate New York publishing firm[1] it's that flexibility and motion are key. Always be moving. Never stop. That's why beneath my khakis you will find a pair of Nike running shoes.

Also because I forgot my saddle oxfords. But still.

Do you see how I took a negative (forgetting to pack my dress shoes) and turned it into a positive (the Nikes being a symbol for my, you know, *mobility*)? That's the kind of thing I do on a regular basis, and that's the kind of thing I want to teach you to do.

What Really Matters

This book isn't about the quality of your writing or your music. It's not about the depth of your message and is, in fact, not about your message at

[1] Our mailing address was actually Altoona, PA.

all. This book is about what really matters: how many people you know and, *ergo*, how many of those people will buy your product.

This book is about growing your platform for the sake of your platform. Because the more people who know you—and by "know you" I mean follow you on some form of social media—the more important you are. And, I would even argue, the *better* you are.

"How do I quantify 'better'?" you may ask. Well, it varies by individual. For me, tonight, it means a comped room at the Holiday Inn Express in Carbondale, Illinois and a free steak dinner courtesy of the founders of "Know Everybody 2014: A Conference on Marketing, Web Design, and Small Engine Repair." It means happy hour in the lobby with hot hors d'oeuvres. Sound nice? If you want to live like me—like a business rock-star who lives like an actual rock star—then get out there and do what matters. Grow your platform.

CHAZ-RONYMS

At the end of each chapter, I will provide you with a chaz-ronym™ to help you remember the practical lessons we've covered.

What is a chaz-ronym™, you might ask? It's a word I made up to describe a business-term that is comprised of the first letter of a bunch of other words. They are meant to be short, pithy reminders of how readers can succeed in business and networking. Chaz-ronyms are perfect for reproduction on those small, rubbery wrist bands, and will be available for a limited time on a larger, sleeve-sized band, containing all fourteen chaz-ronyms. (Notice how I keep saying *chaz-ronym*? That's on purpose.) Here's a sample chaz-ronym:

PUTTING
LEVERAGE
AND
TENACITY
FOR
ORGANIZATIONAL
REFORM
MANAGEMENT

February 9-11
Davenport, IA
Civic Center

MEGA
1998

CHAPTER 1

Presenter • Exhibitor • Booth B6

I Have More Twitter Followers
Than You, Which Means,
Implicitly, More People Care
About Me Than Care About You,
Which Obviously Means
My Book Is Better Than Yours

I'll never forget the day my agent[2] told me to get a Facebook page. He told me that it's yet another way to get my important message out there, and yet another way to connect with "my public." I was skeptical. I told him "Facebook is for teenage girls," to which he replied, "Yeah, but they're potential business book buyers." That's when it clicked for me. That's also when I started getting "pokes" from lots of girls named Brittani who spell it with the "I" at the end and attend Lansing Community College on a part-time basis.

A Subheading about Agents

Having an agent is essential. I used to think that having an agent was only for professional athletes, actors, and writers . . . but now I want to impress upon you the value of EVERYONE having an agent. For example, my accountant has an agent. My father, who is a shoe salesman, has an agent. My agent actually has his own agent. Having an agent gives you two very important things:

1.   The ability to say "I have an agent."

---

[2] See also: things I like being able to say.

2. The ability to say "You'll have to talk to my agent."

They also perform services like contract nego-tiation and sometimes go to parent/teacher conferences I don't feel like attending. Imagine the look of impressed surprise on my son's teacher's face when I informed her that my agent would be representing me at parent/teacher conferences.

My agent also, sometimes, handles my personal correspondence. So if instead of a Christmas card, you receive a form letter on elegant, 25% cotton agency letterhead, you'll know it's from me and you'll know that I empowered my agent to sign all Christmas letters as me.

The Look of an Agent

It's important that your agent look the part. I require my guy to wear double-breasted suits, Borsalino hats[3] and cufflinks at all times. I require him to slick back his hair in the fashion of Pat Riley, who is better known as the coach of the

---

[3] I have no idea what this is.

Showtime-era Los Angeles Lakers, a team I followed from my courtside seats[4]. I also require him to call me on my mobile phone three times per day, just so that I can raise my index finger and say, "It's my agent, I need to take this." I will then start shouting large numbers into the phone in order to impress whomever I'm with. This has never failed to impress a room full of people.

Throughput

Ever heard of the term "throughput?" I didn't think so. That's because I just coined it. I made it up on the golf course, as sort of a pastiche of "play through" and "putt." I'm copyrighting it and making it a key plank in my business platform. *What is throughput*, you might ask?

It doesn't matter. What does matter is that as a Business Leader, it's important to always be making up new, nebulous terms that can mean a variety of things to a variety of people[5].

---

[4] I sat courtside once, in 1993, when they were playing the Milwaukee Bucks. I was a guest of Michael Regency, back when we were on speaking terms.

[5] Varieties of people are also known, in business-ese, as "Tribes."

Whole-ocracy

This is another one of those terms that someone made up. In their case, it was Google, which is a leading Internet search engine and also a very successful company. Personally, I have an exclusive rights merchandising deal with the search engine Alta Vista™ which means that every time I'm searching the web, I'm doing it through their engine. Needless to say, I get a lot of hits on things that were produced pre- 1999. This Ricky Martin guy is a riot . . . and I'm having a lot of fun trying to decide on my favorite Spice Girl. Also, this James Cameron *Titanic* picture looks absolutely unbelievable.

> **"In their case, it was Google, which is a leading Internet search engine and also a very successful company."**

A Whole-ocracy is the idea that everyone's idea matters in a company, and that no one man is more valuable than another. This sounds like a load of touchy-feely [expletive] to me.

The Point

Throughput and *Whole-ocracy* are only relevant if they're allowing you to do what matters most: acquiring a platform, and by a platform I mean followers, and by followers I mean people who visit your social media pages and click "like" or "follow." These people matter because they contribute to a number that represents *your* value.

Here's what I mean, tangibly: If I have 77,000 Twitter followers, and you only have 4,000, it means I'm better than you. "Better how?" you might ask. Better by 73,000. The ability to put a numeric value on human lives is an absolute Revolutionary, Paradigm-shifting, Leader-shifting Proposition.

It means that I'm better. Numerically. Quantifiably. It means that my book is better than yours, and it means that regardless of the fact that you used to beat me up in high school and stuff me into my locker, I am better than you[6].

---

[6] That's for you, [name omitted], you [expletive] [expletive] mother [expletive].

CHAPTER 1
CHAZ-RONYM!

MEDIA

MAKING

ENERGETIC,

DIPLOMATIC

INTERNET

ALGORITHMS

February 9-11
Davenport, IA
Civic Center

MEGA
1998

CHAPTER 2

Presenter • Exhibitor • Booth B6

Something Vague About Leadership,
In Which the Words "Leader" and "Ship"
Are Somehow Manipulated in a Creative
Way . . . Possibly (Absolutely) Integrating
the Word "Shift" and also Incorporating
the Words "Intentional" and "Drift."

And "Paradigms."

Part 1: Shift

Shifting is what you do if you're a cutting-edge leader. Here's the thing: nobody wants to lead something and have it stay the same, unless that thing is the Green Bay Packers, the New England Patriots, or Head and Shoulders.

If you're leading anything else, you need to shift it. What does "shifting it" mean? It often means making a new logo. Or getting a new author photo taken. Or taking a trip to Tahiti with your expense account and calling it a "planning retreat." Or creating a new website for your company. Or firing some people. At any rate, the leader who isn't "shifting" is dying.

Part 2: Drift

Drifting is more than something I do occasionally in my late-model Honda, while wearing a shiny shirt and lots of hair gel. Drifting is not only an occasional killer of teenage boys who like to drag race. It's a killer of companies and corporate identities.

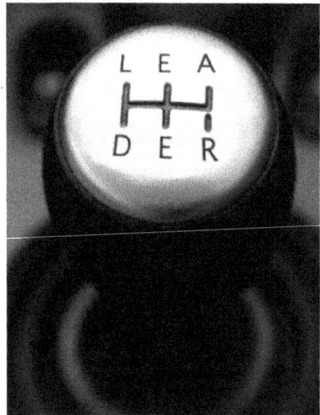

Leadershift! Get it?

What is "drift?" It's not shifting. Shifting is intentional, and things that are intentional are good. Drifting is not-intentional. It's what happens you momentarily lose control of your Honda, or when you buy an unlicensed yacht, invite a girl you've known for a few weeks on a romantic interlude, and then end up being found three days later dehydrated and in shock, by the US Coast Guard. Think of your company in the same way. Your company is a guy in an unlicensed yacht, drifting around in the ocean with a girl of questionable character who ended up being not all that interesting. You get the point.

Drift is when you start out with one goal or mission, and then find yourself doing something completely different.

Part 3: Paradigms

We don't know what they are, other than they're being shifted (and occasionally deconstructed). If you happen to shift a paradigm and then something good happens, you become a Revolutionary. This is good. This is something to highlight when you get your next batch of business cards printed. If you happen to shift a paradigm and then something bad happens you will need to . . .

Part 4: Reinvent Yourself

Reinventing oneself is a tool in every business executive's metaphorical toolbox[7]. If your business isn't working, blow it up and start over. Often this happens on an idea level, where new business plans and mission statements are written.

Once, it involved actually blowing up my business, which is a rather long story that I'm legally obligated to not go into at this particular time.

---

[7] Which is, in itself, a very awkward metaphor. Stay with me.

CHAPTER 2
CHAZ-RONYM!

LEGENDARY

ENERGY

AND

DETERMINATION

February 9-11
Davenport, IA
Civic Center

MEGA
1998

CHAPTER 3

Presenter • Exhibitor • Booth B6

The One About "Change"
And How It's "Everything"

I once said, "The more things change, the more they stay the same." I've since seen that slogan all over certain t-shirts and bumper stickers, prompting me to bring lawsuits against no less than 29 different corporate entities—many of which (lawsuits) are still pending in local or federal courts of law. The point? Change is the only constant, which is another slogan I invented.

Subheading Are Also Everything

Before we talk about "change" as a core concept, I would be remiss if I didn't first discuss the importance of Subheadings. Subheadings are great for the kinds of fast-paced, type-A people who read business books. These are people who don't necessarily have time to wait until the next paragraph to figure out what's in it. That's why you need a subheading to tell them. Because Time is Money[8].

Because here's the thing: without the subheading, your reader may not be smart enough to know what they're reading about. I like to try to use subheadings two to three times per page.

---

[8] I made this up.

Here's an example of how I use subheadings in other realms of life:

<u>The Grocery List</u>

Meats:

☐ ½ pound of ground beef.
☐ Two packages of skinless, boneless chicken.
☐ Canned tuna.

Drinks:

☐ Four bottles, Soda Stream™ syrup.
☐ One gallon skim milk.
☐ One box, cabernet sauvignon.

And so forth. The list, instead of just being six mixed-together bullet points, has been broken into manageable sets of three.

The Next Paragraph, On Change

I embrace change. The thing about change is that if you're constantly changing your focus or approach, you never have to be accountable for anything. Change is organic.

Short Departure on Being Organic

"Organic" used to mean "relating to or derived from living matter." Now, thanks to me and how I started using it in the late 1990s, the word "organic" is used in any number of business contexts, including but not limited to: how ideas can be organic, how companies can be organic, how conversations can be organic, how team-work can be organic, how this book developed organically, how actual organs (bodily and musical) can be organic, and finally (and back to the topic at hand) how change can be organic.

The point is that though you can't really explain it, and in fact can't explain it at all, being organic is a good thing.

"'Organic' used to mean 'relating to or derived from living matter.'"

And this word is in no way "played" or "over" as some would suggest. To me, the word "organic" is just organically evolving.

More on Change

Change is a part of life. I've changed my own personal look several times. What follows is a list of the personas I've embraced over the last five to seven years:

- Competitive mountain biker.

- Amway rep.

- Freelance web designer.

- Third degree black belt, North American Combat Federation.

- Independent record producer.

- Seminary student.

- Urban farmer.

- Homeschool father.

The point is that if you're not a radical change agent . . . you're . . . um . . . part of the problem or something. Because being into the status quo, or doing things the way they've always been done, is for people who are lame and uninteresting.

CHAPTER 3
CHAZ-RONYM!

NEW

NEVER

EXISTING

WORKPLACE

My Author Photo Was Taken
in Such a Way as to Make Me Look
Equal Parts Credible, Aggressive, Sexy,
Compassionate, Thoughtful, Maverick-y,
and Well-Dressed.

Also, Check Out My Hair.

When you're an author who is also a social media and marketing expert, your author photo is everything. It goes on the back flap of your books, it goes on your business card, it goes on the strange filmy "wrap" thing that you encase your Acura Integra in, it goes on the flyers you occasionally leave at Denny's instead of a tip, and it also goes on the billboard off of South MLK Boulevard which advertises your upcoming speaking engagement in Ballroom C of the Ramada Inn by the airport. That said, I can't overstate how important this is. I actually had a batch of these taken six years before I had my first book deal.

In fact, when I was in grade school I implored the school district photographer to let me drape my sport jacket over my shoulder, jauntily. He also let me experiment with some other "business casual" poses before we settled on a shot that featured me sitting behind the Principal's mahogany desk. When you're a future business tycoon, these are the kinds of things you do.

When you finally sign that book deal with Moody, Baker, Thomas Nelson, FaithWords, or Bethany House, they'll ask you to send in several hi-res author photos. They'll discuss using these on bookmarks, coasters, flyers, life-sized posters, vinyl blow-up dolls, and all kinds of other printed materials that have absolutely no correlation to how well your book sells and which you'll have to move out of your basement when you decide to downsize several years later.

Size of Smile as Relates to Effectiveness of Author Photo

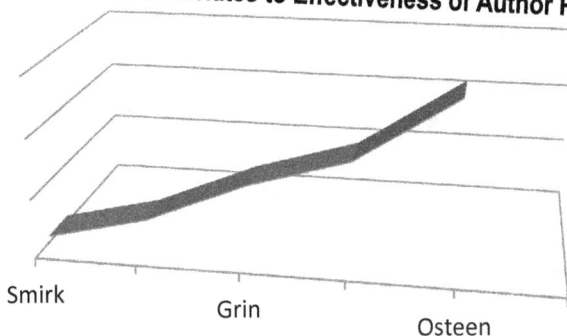

Smirk   Grin   Osteen

Someone in your publisher's marketing department will be convinced that these things are all a good idea. He or she will usually have moved to another company, gotten married, or decided to go to graduate school before your book even comes out (not that I'm bitter).

My current author photo is an object lesson in sexy, credible, maverick-ness. If my author photo were an animal, it would be a sleek panther stalking its prey through a wooded mountain-side, except in this analogy I am the panther and the wooden mountainside is just the marketplace in general. If I were you, I would initially shoot (metaphorically-speaking) for being a more accessible animal, like a golden retriever or a lemur. You have to be a realist.

"My current author photo is an object lesson in sexy, credible, maverick-ness." My photo will take you to previously - unheard - of heights of marketing and business credibility. Just seeing my picture will make you want to buy what-ever product it is I'm championing. My photo will blow your mind.

Here are some suggested locations for your author shot:

- A mountaintop (subtext: I am the king of the mountain, as it were.)

- Your office, provided your office has lots of mahogany, and many pictures of you standing next to celebrities. Also, lots of framed degrees and awards. If your office lacks these things, proceed to another suggested location.

- Surrounded by poor people (subtext: I have a big heart).

- The Nike campus in Beaverton, Oregon (before they call security).

- On the bow of an ocean liner (subtext: this is MY ocean liner, also I am a fan of James Cameron's *Titanic* though if I had been driving it would have been deftly maneuvered through the icebergs and safely to shore)

Divergent Philosophies on Smiling

Your smile shouldn't be too wide, openhearted, or authentic, lest you look somehow vapid and trivial. Your smile should be slightly wry—it should be the kind of smile that says "I just stole 25 of Michael Regency's Twitter followers, and it's not even lunchtime" or "after Bill Hybels fired me as his marketing advisor, I may or may not have broken the jaw of the security guy who got a little rough with me on the way out of the Willow Creek Fayetteville Campus." It should be the kind of smile that says, "I was only two interviews away from being named President of Cedarville College in 1998."

Frowning

You shouldn't frown either, because frowning suggests that you may be unhappy or, worse, not in control of every situation all of the time. Frowning suggests that you may not be entirely convinced of your own awesomeness. This cannot be.

Also Avoid . . .

- Family. Having family members in your photos suggests weakness, and also suggests that you'll let calls go to voicemail on your daughter's special day. Your clients need to know that you're there for them 24 hours a day, even if your wife is having a non-invasive outpatient surgery, which according to WebMD shouldn't even be a big deal.

- Creativity. Again, creativity and originality are for the weak-minded. What your clients need to know is that you're rock-solid, steady, and secure. They need to know that you're an unshakable rock, like the Government and the stock market.

- The colors purple and teal.

- The temptation to remove your glasses and sort of nibble on the end of them thoughtfully. I ruined a good pair of glasses in a photo shoot by doing this.

- The temptation to use the selfie that you took at Shaquille O'Neal's retirement party as your author photo. I learned this the hard way.

- Baseball caps (unless you're LeCrae, Trip Lee, or a professional baseball player).

- Women (unless you are a woman).

CHAPTER 4
CHAZ-RONYM!

HAVING

AGGRESSIVE

INTELLIGENT

RESOURCES

February 9-11
Davenport, IA
Civic Center

MEGA
1998

CHAPTER 5

Presenter · Exhibitor · Booth B6

More People Means
You're More Successful:
How Implementing This Core Value in
Your Church, Family, and Para-Church
Ministry Can Make All the Difference

Who's In Your Tribe?

Your tribe is comprised of the people who follow you. Meaning, more specifically, the people who are your "friends" or "followers" on social media. It's important to call this group of people your "tribe" because this is a business term that is trending right now[9]. Make no mistake about it, the word "tribes" is not just some contrived marketing gimmick by some author, contrived specifically for the purpose of moving product or even for the purpose of just creating a different word for "audience" or "customers" because it's somehow become too passé and modern-era to refer to the people who buy your stuff as "customers." No way. The concept of tribes has been around since Europeans discovered Native Americans. Actually maybe before, according to some sources[10].

Tribal Secret

How do you get a tribe? The secret is that it doesn't matter. Only that there is a lot of people in your tribe. They can be there for a variety of

---

[9] And might be obsolete by the time I'm finished with this chapter.

[10] Ex: Wikipedia.

reasons ranging from actual interest in you or your product, to the free "MEGA" t-shirts you gave out at the "Regional Conference on Getting Noticed and Excellence in Creative Nonfiction." Either way, they're now in your tribe. The more people you have, the more successful you are. You can have several Tribes, containing different people. In fact, you should.

Also, I would be remiss if I didn't mention that sometimes you get a tribe when your Cessna Citation runs out of fuel over a certain remote section of Peru, having been re-routed by Terminal Control when you were trying to fly yourself to the Bears/Colts Super Bowl in Miami a few years ago. Sometimes you are taken in by indigenous peoples and subjected to certain awkward medical experiments[11] until you are eventually assimilated and made an honorary member just before your agent sends a rescue helicopter. This can happen. Sometimes you end up buying their land for pennies on the dollar and

"Sometimes you get a tribe when your Cessna Citation runs out of fuel over a certain remote section of Peru."

---

[11] Some of which involved my "swimsuit area."

creating a coffee plantation, which you then turn around and sell at a tidy sum to a large and recognizable American gas-station-and-donut chain. This is another[12] way to acquire a tribe.

This is also the reason why I didn't tweet between the months of January and April in 2011.

Size Matters

All of the best things in the world are big. For example, New York City[13] has more people in it than almost any other city, which means that it's better. Also, my 2003 Cadillac Deville has more cylinders in its Northstar Engine than, say, a Toyota Prius. This makes it a better car. Also, my considerable height (I'm 6'4") and my regal mountain of hair makes me, essentially, better than the many men who are shorter than I am. You get the idea.

---

[12] (albeit more literal)

[13] Where I ran a traditional publishing house for three years. At the behest of Gut Check Legal, I'm required to tell you that our address was actually in Altoona, PA.

The Idea, In Case You Didn't Get It

The idea here is that numbers are the only metric that matters. Want to know how you're doing in pastoral ministry? Count the number of people in your church or youth group. Or better yet, just consider your budget, provided the number is large enough to provide fulfillment and the feeling that you're doing a good job.

Want to know how you're doing as a parent? Simply count the number of children (adopted or biological) living in your home. Want to know how you're doing as a husband? Your only metric should be the number of years that you've been married . . . and if you've been married a long time you can be smug and superior about this, lording it over others who haven't been married as long.

Numbers are Everything

Numbers are the new letters.
Numbers are the new character.

Because, as I alluded to in the subheading just four lines above this one, Numbers are Everything.

CHAPTER 5
CHAZ-RONYM!

TERRIFIC

RESOURCES

IN

BECOMING

EXCELLENT

February 9-11
Davenport, IA
Civic Center

MEGA
1998

CHAPTER 6

Presenter • Exhibitor • Booth B6

Why Yes, I Did Just Have
My Teeth Whitened.

How Sweet of You to Notice.

This chapter is about the appearance of humility. Because here's the thing: When you're an ultra-successful business maverick who is also leading several tribes and shifting a number of paradigms in creative ways, you'll receive lots of compliments. Therefore, you'll need to develop the ability to appear humble.

Here are the steps to appearing to be humble:

1. Act like you're surprised by the compliment. Sometimes when I'm feeling blue I'll put on my most expensive suit and wear it to run-of-the-mill public places. Often, people will say things like, "Wow, you really dressed up for an afternoon out at Wal-Mart," to which I'll reply, "Oh, this? It's nothing . . . it's just that I have an important business meeting for my traditional New York Publishing House[14] as soon as I drop this 14 gallon drum of olive oil off at my condo." It's at this point that the person gets very impressed.

---

[14] Named, "Traditional New York Publishing House" or "TNYPH" on the New York Stock Exchange (NYSE) (forthcoming). Also, I am again legally obligated to remind you that our mailing address is Altoona, PA.

2. Deflect the compliment, by complimenting someone else. When someone makes an observation to me such as, "It looks like you just had your teeth whitened because they are radiant," I'll often reply by saying, "My tooth guy is the best. He does all of Tom Wopat's tooth work as well. Also, Tom Wopat was the dark-haired guy on *The Dukes of Hazzard*."

3. Just slap the person on the back and continue smiling radiantly.

4. Ask them if they'd like a signed glossy publicity photo and a flyer about your new book.

5. Subtly try and see if they're doing anything for dinner and, if not, if they'd be willing to treat you to dinner so that you can tell them about your timeshare in Orlando (see: Chapter 10).

A Certain Rock Star Quality

People often say to me, "Chaz, you have a certain rock star quality about you," to which I smile and deflect the compliment while also at the same time completely basking in it. I then go on to tell them that I launched and then took-advantage-of a flagship program in the 1990s, wherein for a flat fee of $400 the rock band Petra would let you be their guitarist on tour for two months. For me, that involved playing a total of three church youth group shows in church basements. But the experience was priceless.

When I walked out onto that stage underneath the basketball hoop in the multi-purpose room, I felt alive in ways that I'd never felt before. When I felt the white-hot glare of what I thought was a spotlight but what turned out to be a reflection off the youth pastor's bald head, I knew that I was born to be a rock star.

As it turned out, that $400 check bounced and John Schlitt may or may not have thrown me off the back of a moving tour bus. Either way, the experience was profound and formative, and I've lived like a Rock Star ever since. For me, this involves:

- Chartering a limo, even if it sometimes doesn't make any sense to anyone. If you learn only one thing from this humble volume, let it be this: It's important to arrive certain places—a posh new restaurant, a book launch, your child's grade school—in a limo from time to time, as it sends the right kind of message to your constituents.

- Wearing sunglasses everywhere . . . even inside. Sunglasses can serve a practical purpose like shielding your eyes from the sun, or covering a black eye you sustained in a scuffle with Michael Regency. But they also let people know that you have a certain rock star quality about you, and should be treated as such.

- Having a "rider." A rider is a list of things you need in the "Green Room" at every tour stop or speaking location along your route. At the apex of my career, my rider included: A brand new DVD player and a sealed copy of *The Karate Kid,* four thousand dollars in unmarked bills in a new leather briefcase, six Ashton Maduros, an unopened event golf shirt, a filet-mignon dinner, and a cocker-spaniel puppy. Today, my more modest rider includes: a bottle of water and a ride to the airport.

Event Rider for Chaz Held-Marriot

Speaker. Leader. Visionary. Spokesman.

Contact WOW-ZA! Talent and Booking with any questions. (5██████9 www.geocities.com/getchazzy

---

DRESSING ROOM:

Chaz's dressing room is to be a haven and sanctuary from any negative energy or depressing reality. To that end, only good smells, sights, and sounds are allowed within. Only attractive people should interact with Mr. Marriot before, during, and after the event, and only in a fawning way. In addition, please provide the following:

Four full-length mirrors
3 Leather couches
A sealed bucket of BULL-STRENGTH supplement
        (now banned by FDA—please locate on black market beforehand)
28 bottles of spring water that has never been warm or frozen
48 Bath-sized soft cotton towels
Brown M & Ms. (just brown ones)
Glossy photo of Mark-Paul Gosselaar (for hair reference)
Unopened copy of the Karate Kid DVD
Cocker Spaniel puppy (previously unpetted)
2 boxes of Kleenex (one with lotion, one without)

Above: Excerpt from mid-90s rider.
Below: Example of one of my current riders.

- BOTTLE OF WATER
- RIDE TO AIRPORT
- DON'T ASK ABOUT MY BLACK EYE, OR MICHAEL REGENCY (OR MY NIKES)

- ASK ABOUT MY NIKES!

Hyphenated Last Names

In the late 1990s I hyphenated my last name for two years, because hyphenated last names focus grouped really well, and I have a tendency to base *all* of my decisions on how things focus group, because really the only reality is that which has been vetted by a focus group. As a result, some of my books and websites bear the name Chaz Held-Marriot.

Granted, it wasn't a legal name change, rather, just something I did in publishing. Also, I was married for less than 30 days under that name, a marriage which was recognized and then later annulled in Reno, Nevada. All of that to say, I don't recommend, in today's business climate, hyphenating your last name, unless you're writing in the Liberal Female Theologians marketplace.

The Motivational Poster Initiative

One thing that I think is absolutely critical to every business venture is the quality of the motivational posters in and around the office. If I've learned one thing it's that when you couple a vague motivational term like "Determination" with a picture of something equally vague but picturesque, like a mountain, great things can happen motivationally and also people can momentarily forget that they're sitting in a cubicle underneath a life-sucking fluorescent light, entering data for an office that processes the sale of Peruvian coffee to large American gas station chains.

People also like being reminded to "Hang in There" via a photograph of a cat hanging from the limb of a tree. I have a copy of this poster hanging on the wall in my studio apartment, right next to a "Division of Chores" list that I made with my roommate, Mr. Segal. On especially lonely nights you may find yourself gazing at that **"I think this is normal."** poster and sobbing uncontrollably. I think this is normal. I think Steve Jobs did this with a similar cat poster in his home.

Break Rooms and Motivational Art

Perhaps the most critical place to display your motivational art is the break room. In addition to a sad arrangement of tables and a microwave, your break room needs to feature photographs of impoverished children from Third World countries. Studies have shown that companies who display this kind of art—thereby perpetrating the idea that they have a quote-unquote social conscience—do 17% better in terms of profit and loss.

There is, apparently, an interesting motivational link between impoverished-yet-still-somewhat-proud-and-beautiful indigenous peoples and the rates of productivity in mostly white, suburban office workers.

Who knew?

CHAPTER 6
CHAZ-RONYM!

HAVING

OUTRAGEOUS

TRAJECTORIES

MEGA
1998

February 9-11
Davenport, IA
Civic Center

CHAPTER 7

Presenter • Exhibitor • Booth B6

"When I Wake Up In the Morning
I Just Can't Shake the Feeling of Emptiness
I Have When I Think About the Fact That,
In Spite of All My Social Media, All My
Money, All of the Mid-Level Luxury Sedans
I've Owned, All of My Speaking
Engagements, All of the Nonprofit Boards
I'm the Chair Of, All of the Conferences
I've Keynoted, and All of the Times I've
Tried to Golf While Smoking a Cohiba,
I'm Just a Scared Little Boy Trying to
Prove Something to My Father"

When I was a child and adolescent, in school, I had this problem wherein whenever I would get anxious (which was all the time), my face would sort of get all flushed and hot so that even if it wasn't necessarily even hot outside (or inside), it would look like I was hot because of how red my face was. This led to lots of avoidance activities, like trying to make my body cold (by wearing less clothing in the winter) so that my face wouldn't flush.

Also, it led to me eating lunch by myself because, for whatever reason, the lunchroom at my high school (and also at college) was a trigger for the face-flushing. I became accustomed to stealthily finding and then sitting-by air-conditioning registers (summer) and avoiding heaters (winter). It goes without saying that I failed to start any companies or open any offshore bank accounts during this period of time.

For years this was debilitating. It meant that from roughly fourth grade through like my sophomore year of college, I avoided talking to girls, and avoiding serving on committees or in any other context that would put me directly in front of other people in a talking capacity because being in front of other people and having those people look at me would cause the face-flush to happen.

Another thing that caused it was my barber shop back home in Empty Factory, Indiana[15]. The setup of this particular shop was that the barber's chair (which was positioned right in front of the big mirror and all the multi-colored vats of Barbicide with all the floating combs) looked out on a semi-circle of chairs which, on any given day, would be filled with all manner of jaded farmers and factory workers who would be staring at me while I had my hair cut. This resulted in an almost debilitating level of anxiety.

VAX: Becoming Awesome

The personal transformation of Chaz Marriot began to happen in college when I realized that, after two years of eating lunch barricaded in my room, I would need to begin meeting people if I was ever to realize my dream of becoming a

---

[15] This is the actual name. The Chamber of Commerce has done a lot to try and work with this, in a marketing capacity, but to little avail. The Empty Factory Festival was a flop, as was the "See The Inside of an Abandoned Warehouse" initiative. Also a failure was the attempt to launch an "arts district." However, the town has found new life by leasing all of the empty factories to Emergent™ Churches for their worship gatherings.

sought-after expert in the world of Social Media[16] and Marketing.

I logged onto our school's primitive VAX system, where I found comfort behind the protective barrier of the computer screen where I could meet people in an environment that didn't involve the actual meeting of actual people.

I began sending out VAX messages under an assumed name, which (proto-emails) contained practical helps for students groups trying to market their goods and services. I became something of an underground VAX legend, which is why I still use that system for my personal correspondence.

Walking a Little Taller

Suddenly, I began to walk a little taller. Also, full disclosure: I grew six inches between my sophomore and junior year, which may explain the walking taller. Being tall gave me the sense that I was better than people who were short. I realized that being better than others was a feeling I wanted more of.

---

[16] This didn't exist yet.

I stopped leaving class early. The face-flushing problem would eventually subside, and it would only happen in the weight room, where I regularly astounded my classmates with my feats of strength (like bench-pressing 405 pounds). I began lifting weights as a means to filling out the finished cuffs of short - sleeved conference golf shirts, but I found solace and community in the weight room. In fact, my first full-time marketing client was BULL STRENGTH™ a company that specialized in the import/export/distillation of authentic veterinary-grade bull semen as an FDA-approved anabolic nutritional[17] supplement[18].

"Being tall gave me the sense that I was better than people who were short."

Once BULL STRENGTH went public, all my dreams started coming true. I married a girl I met in the gym, and with whom I started an actual face-to-face conversation when I complimented

---

[17] Tagline: "Perform Like a Bull in Appropriate Contexts which We'll Leave Up to You to Interpret!"

[18] Use at your own risk. May result in certain undesirable side-effects including, but not limited to excessive body hair growth, massive liver failure, howling at the moon, and charging through certain kinds of wooden fences.

her Detroit Pistons workout shorts. It all grew from there. It turned out that the girl was a gifted and prodigious writer who couldn't seem to write more than two sentences at any given time. But those two sentences were brilliant. Little did we both know that this would become a huge competitive advantage years later with the advent of Twitter.

An early banner ad mock-up I made for BULL STRENGTH supplements. I am still unclear as to why it was rejected.

Still, there was an emptiness that I felt could only be filled through the purchase of several luxury sedans and, ultimately, a time share in the (then) fastest-growing suburb of Orlando. I wanted to feel as though I had really made it and the leather and replicated wood-grain inside my luxury sedan temporarily gave that feeling.

Still, I couldn't shake the feeling of emptiness. So I bought a golf course and tried to fight Michael Regency near the cash bar at the "2006 Regional Conference on Being Popular" at Calvin College.

The golf course turned out to be a bad idea. The fist-fight did too, but less-so.

Finding Contentment

I have closed the golf course to the public, and it is currently an ultra-exclusive Country Club in which I am the only member[19]. I play seventy-two holes a day[20], and have perfected the art of using the shaft of my driver to ash my Cohiba on the backswing. There are YouTube videos of this online if you're interested in seeing how it works. I also gave a well-attended breakout talk about this entitled "Differing Perspectives on Ashing Your Cohiba with the Shaft of Your Driver."

There's a certain proud gracefulness in playing golf by yourself day after day. Still, I sometimes ask myself: "Where is the happiness" and "Why isn't my father here telling me how well I'm doing and how much he admired the seven-iron I

---

[19] I call it "The Courtyard by Marriot" as a play on my last name.

[20] I'm currently selling opportunities to play golf with me and talk business. If interested, email **chaz.marriot@gutchekpress.com** and include the words "Golfing with Chaz" in the subject line. Someone from my tribe will be in touch with you regarding pricing and scheduling.

hit on the 13th hole, the one with the water hazard and the nasty dog-leg?"

I just need to hear this from my father.

CHAPTER 7
CHAZ-RONYM

SUDDEN

ABJECT

DEPRESSION

February 9-11
Davenport, IA
Civic Center

MEGA
1998

CHAPTER 8

Presenter • Exhibitor • Booth B6

An Archival List of All the Famous
People I've Been Photographed Next to
In the (Unlikely) Event That I'm No
Longer Able to Pay Rent on My Office
Space and Something Happens
to the Pictures

Bill Hybels. This guy is amazing. He owns a 20,000 seat arena, a Christian barbershop, four Christian cafés, a bookstore, a recording studio, a gym, a karate dojo, and a petting zoo—all under one roof! Also, he's a pastor.

Rachel Held-Evans. She's gotten huffy and indignant about three issues and posted thirty-seven Tweets in the time it's taken you to read this sentence. And that, in a nutshell, is why she's amazing.

Mark Driscoll. You know that old adage that says, "Money can't buy either happiness or a place on the *New York Times* bestseller list?" I posit that it can, and give you, as evidence, Mark Driscoll (not about the happiness). It may or may not have been my marketing company (which is itself a subsidiary of a large multi-national defense contractor) that advised Driscoll to buy his way onto the NYT list. (Note: I very publicly expelled Driscoll from my picture collection—via blogosphere and Twitter—after the Driscoll Controversey of 2014, an act which garnered me four new Twitter followers. i.e., net gain = 3).

Brian McLaren. Yes, those are our kimonos.

Rick Warren. His church was running a special where if you send in a digital photo and $99 he would Photoshop you in. I've never actually met Warren, but I feel a certain kinship to him, philosophically.

Michael Regency. We've been great ever since he forgave me for fighting him at a conference in 2006 (long story).

Frank Turk. Certain people get that "Hey, aren't you Frank Turk?" look in their eye whenever they see . . . Frank Turk. Or the guy who played George Costanza in *Seinfeld*.

Rob Bell. Yes, those are our surfboards, and yes, that is the rest of the cast of Rob's ill-fated television pilot.

The lead singer of Stryper. Or Cyndi Lauper . Hard to tell in the picture . . .

Tullian Tchvi . . . [sic] **dja . . .** [sic] **a . . .** [sic]

Tim Tebow. He's the one kneeling in the end zone at Moody / Lifeway / Crossway/Mile High Stadium...that's me in section 8, row 13, in the Broncos jersey.

LeCrae. Not the black rapper . . . the French pastry chef from Naperville. He's a great guy . . . our kids play travel baseball together.

LeCrae. The rapper. I do all of his social media. People tell me I have a gift for sounding like an inner-city hype man with strong Reformed leanings.

Tim Challies. I'm beginning to think there's a better-than-average chance that popular book reviewer Tim Challies doesn't actually exist . . . and that *I* am actually Tim Challies. Which begs the question: Who the [expletive] is this other guy in the picture?!

CHAPTER 8
CHAZ-RONYM!

FOREVER

ABOUT

MAKING

EXECUTIVES

MEGA
1998

February 9-11
Davenport, IA
Civic Center

CHAPTER 9

Presenter · Exhibitor · Booth B6

Family First: And By "First" I Mean
I Speak With Each of My Children
Once a Year,
And Only on Their Birthdays

It's important to leverage family.

Family sells. Look at every successful sitcom besides Cheers, Seinfeld, 30 Rock, and Night Court . . . they all involve families. But family can also be a serious drain on your time and financial resources. I learned this the hard way when, instead of buying a bike for my son on his birthday, I invested the money in a series of banner ads heralding my new talk series. I gave him, instead, a copy of my new hardcover book. He seemed less than thrilled but was a good sport about it.

JC Penny's Handsome

If you have a family, it's important that they look perfect. They need to be preferably blonde, and very attractive, in the vein of JC Penny's models from the late 1980s. Your sons need to look like they're on their way to a tennis tournament, and your daughters need to be unbelievably attractive, but not in any way that could be construed as sexual. They need to look like the covers of Christian romance novels from the 1980s.

This Sentence About Bo Derek

Your wife needs to look like Bo Derek, if Bo Derek were dressed in a very conservative sweater.

The most important thing about your family is the new photo you'll have taken of them every six months. This photo will be posted all over Facebook, Twitter, and the blogosphere, reminding your readers of what a fantastic husband and father you are, when you're not busy being a business tycoon. Because even the greatest business tycoon doesn't want to go home to an empty studio apartment above a dojo after giving a talk at the Webberville Area Chamber of Commerce.

Context is Everything

Family is so key. Family is everything. Family are the people you have around to be impressed when you make a key Business Conquest. Family are the people at whom you hold up your index finger when your agent calls, and you say "I have to take this." Without family there is no one in the room when you receive that important call from your agent telling you that your book is about to be remaindered and would you like to buy the existing inventory for 85% off the cover price.

Family are also the people who are at Christmas. Sometimes I get so lonely in this apartment that I begin talking to the life-sized cardboard cutout of Shaquille O'Neal that I won in a raffle at his retirement party. Then I start crying.

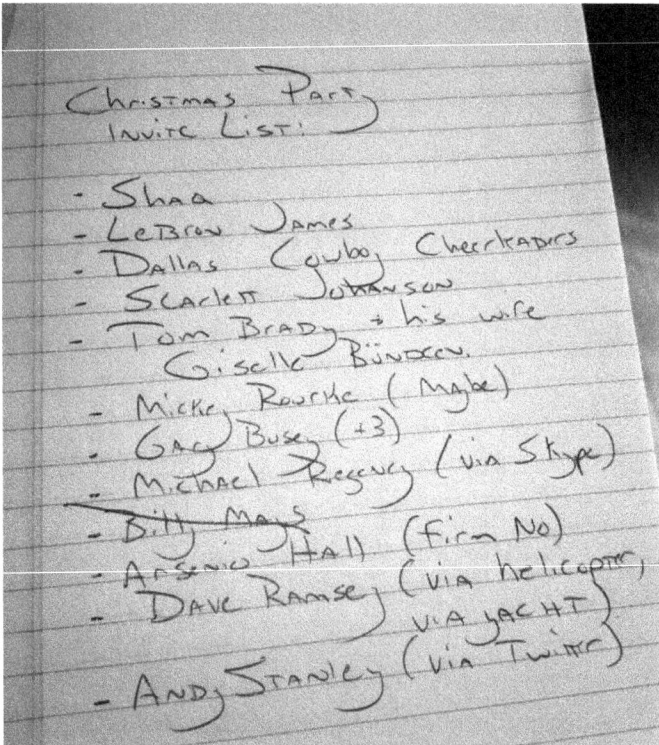

Christmas Party
Invite List:

- Shaq
- LeBron James
- Dallas Cowboy Cheerleaders
- Scarlett Johansson
- Tom Brady + his wife
  Giselle Bündchen.
- Mickey Rourke (Maybe)
- Gary Busey (+3)
- Michael Regency (via Skype)
- Billy Mays
- Arsenio Hall (Firm No)
- Dave Ramsey (via helicopter)
  VIA YACHT
- Andy Stanley (via Twitter)

It's at this point that I bravely wipe away the tears with the cuff of a distressed denim shirt I got at the Wild Goose Festival in 2007. It's at this point that I look in the mirror, bite my lower lip, and then tell myself, "Chaz, you can either curl up on the couch and watch more *Brady Bunch* reruns like a weak, depressed person, or you can open another offshore bank account."

I choose bank account.

CHAPTER 9

CHAZ-RONYM!

KEEPING

INDIRECT

DISCRETIONARY

SUPPORT

Reasons I Think God May Be Calling You To Buy My Timeshare in the Suburbs of Orlando

There's this misnomer circulating that timeshare condominiums are a thing of the 1980s. There are people who believe that a timeshare is nothing more than a sad little two-bedroom apartment in a no-longer-relevant Orlando suburb, adjacent to a Piggly Wiggly Supermarket and an oil change place. With those detractors I couldn't disagree more wholeheartedly.

My timeshare is two weeks of high-end luxury paradise, which includes a small workout facility on-site, laundry, and a lap pool. There is also a golf course a mere fourteen blocks away. A short ninety-minute drive and you're dipping your toes into the Gulf of Mexico. At the end of a long day of golfing, sunbathing, or using the local coffee shop for their Internet, it's back home to my colorful, floral-print sofa, where I pick up the remote and enjoy everything that basic cable has to offer.

You may ask yourself: why wouldn't I just get a hotel room in Orlando, near Disney or Universal Studios? Because when you're a sought-after expert in social media and marketing, it's important to have several residences. And owning a timeshare in Orlando for two weeks in July counts as having another residence.

When you stay in a hotel, you wind up buying nice meals out in many of the upscale eateries that Orlando has to offer. You also have to deal with the awkwardness of having a maid come into your room to clean it and refresh your supplies each day. Who wants to deal with that? Buying my timeshare is just a sound, business decision. It also provides you a connection to lots of famous people whom I've advised over the years.

Here's a short list of people who have been in my timeshare:

Frank Viola. Revolutionary author.

Frank Viola. Minnesota Twins relief pitcher.

Frank Turk. Though that was a surprise to me.

The Conservative Baldwin Brother, whose name escapes me.

Jack Van Impe, back when we used to work out together. He filmed his "eighth member of the European Union" theory in my guest room.

Steven Furtick. He was going to spontaneously mass baptize a bunch of people in the condo association's pool but it wasn't large enough.

Britt Nicole, who sometimes keeps her bike in the condo.

Creed, which is the reason the third couch cushion is severely burned.

Gary Wailin, who was in my living room as a representative of, his words, "A traditional New York publishing house." He then "acquired" sixteen of my book ideas and paid me an advance of $12.37 which is all he had in his wallet. He then ate all of my cereal. To date, none of the books have been published.

Gary Busey, though he was unconscious.

John Schlitt, ironically, working then for the collection agency he had hired to recoup the $400 from me a decade earlier. I gave him the runaround.

Things You Can Say, When You
Own a Timeshare:

"I'm going to my place in Florida."

"I own multiple homes."

"If you don't wake up in the next 48 hours
I'm calling the cops." (to Busey)

CHAPTER 10
CHAZ-RONYM!

COMPREHENSIVE

ONLINE

NETWORKING

DIRECTORIES,

ONGOING

MEGA
1998

February 9-11
Davenport, IA
Civic Center

CHAPTER 11

Presenter • Exhibitor • Booth B6

Just Because I Live in a Studio
Apartment, above a Karate Dojo,
It Doesn't Mean I'm Not a Sought-
After Expert in the World of
Marketing and Social Media

Even though a variety of circumstances led me to sell my 12,000 square foot mansion on a Miami inlet, adjacent to Shaquille O'Neal's house, and even though I now call a studio apartment above a dojo "home," I am still a sought-after expert in the world of marketing and social media.

The studio provides a perfect blank wall in front of which I film my cutting-edge YouTube videos that are about marketing and business. You will want to subscribe to those videos and watch them because they could potentially change your life.

That said, when you're a sought-after expert in marketing and social media, it's important to constantly be inventing certain words or phrases that have application in the world of business. Because as we all know, inventing new words can lead to book deals. Here is a partial list of words I've invented:

Networkth: This cutting-edge, revolutionary word combines "network" and "net-worth." The implication being that if you take the time to "network" you'll increase your "net-worth." Eh?

Spinergy: Another paradigm-shifting word combo, this one combines "spin" and "energy." Energy is, of course, what I always bring to the table. Spin is what I had to do when the media got wind of my fistfight with Michael Regency in 2006 and I had to reinvent my image. Spinning is also what I do two nights a week at the gym, and also what the room did when I had too much punch at Shaquille O'Neal's retirement party . . . after which I woke up shivering and naked in the back of a catering truck.

Satis-Traction: This is the feeling you get when an idea gets "traction" which is another way to say when an idea becomes reality. It is similar to "satisfaction," in that it is, in fact, come to think of it, identical to "satisfaction." I'm in negotiations with The Rolling Stones to do a new song entitled "I Can't Get No Satis-Traction[21]." Stay tuned for updates. I'm also suing an Orlando chiropractor for the term Satis-Traction, which he is using to market a piece of lumbar-rehabilitation machinery.

> **"Because as we all know, inventing new words can lead to book deals."**

---

[21] Ed. Note: One telephone call has been placed to The Rolling Stones. As yet unreturned.

Once I win the lawsuit, I intend to market and sell a similar device myself.

Prototype of my Satis-traction lumbar-rehab gizmo.

Satis-Fraction: This describes the feeling you get when you sell your newly acquired coffee plantation to a large gas station and donut chain, and then buy the mansion adjacent to Shaquille

O'Neal's. It's also how you feel after you upload 1200 photos of said mansion to Facebook so that all of those jerks from high school can see that you really did have potential, and you really would make it, just like Mrs. Elwood used to say—often right before you got a "swirly" from some guys on the football team.

Dissatis-Fraction: This is what you feel when you have to sell said mansion for a fraction of what you paid for it, and then have to spend days in a coffee shop scouring the want-ads for a studio apartment and then have to end up splitting the rent with a man that you feel could possibly be actor Steven Segal.

Status-Function: This is a term you use to gauge your social status at a given function. Status-Function is measured on a scale of 1 (lowest) to 10 (highest). The time you were invited to Scott Stapp's wedding but were seated in a basement hallway with the janitors scored a 2 on the status-function scale. The time that Mike Tyson invited you to walk to the ring with him, before his fight with "Hurricane" Peter McNeely, was a 10.

Electricentricity: People tell me that I have an electric personality. People say things like "Chaz, you light up a room with your presence" and "When Chaz Marriot walks into the room, it sizzles with excitement." People also tell me that I'm "eccentric" when I do things like put on a three-piece suit just to drive to Jiffy Lube to have the oil changed in my 1999 Lexus. I was also called "eccentric" shortly after I fought Michael Regency . . . in addition, admittedly, to being called "absolutely out of control" and "under arrest."

The point? If you're going to succeed in business, you need to have an electric, and eccentric, personality.

CHAPTER 11
CHAZ-RONYM!

DIRECT

OUTRAGE

JUSTIFIES

OBVIOUSNESS

February 9-11
Davenport, IA
Civic Center

MEGA
1998

CHAPTER 12

Presenter • Exhibitor • Booth B6

How to Leverage the Fact That I'm
95% Sure My New Roommate is
Former Actor and Martial Arts Expert
Steven Segal

My new studio apartment is directly above a dojo. Our landlord is also the sensei, which is really convenient because it means we can walk the rent down between classes. He always wants it in cash. My roommate is a tall, husky, swarthy man with a raspy voice and a ponytail. He also has thick fingers. He wears a Gi around the apartment all the time. For these reasons, and many others, I'm 95% certain he is former actor and martial arts expert Steven Segal.

The question is, how to leverage this? This kind of proximity to a real Hollywood Personality is exhilarating. Mr. Segal doesn't say much, and often spends his free time eating gigantic bowls of Ramen noodles and watching *Marked for Death.*

I have offered to take over all of his Internet marketing, which, at this point, consists of a MySpace page he started for his band, "Spinning Backfist," in 2001. I am encouraging him to update his Facebook status and Tweet several times per day. He responds by saying, "I don't know what to say." I tell him that he has a great deal to share with the world,

"My roommate is a tall, husky, swarthy man with a raspy voice and a ponytail. He also has thick fingers."

at which point he usually shuffles away and closes a door. Social media marketing is a process. It's a journey, not a destination.

SPINNING BACKFIST

I have refrained from showing Mr. Segal my spec screenplay about a marketing executive who loses everything and then finds love with a former Miss America contestant, while also saving the world from nuclear threat. It promises to be a non-stop thrill ride, and has a working title of *Hard to Kill*. I have refrained from showing this to Mr. Segal.

I have also refrained from showing him my sitcom spec, which is about a marketing executive who also moonlights as an NBA basketball player. I have Shaquille O'Neal loosely attached to the project. And by "loosely attached" I mean I was present at his retirement party. It's called *Friends*.

Perhaps I simply leverage the relationship by seeing Mr. Segal as, not so much a human being, but a dollar sign. Because when you're about the business of building platform and influence, that's how you view people. The minute I get to know Mr. Segal as a real, sentient human being with feelings, emotions, lots of laundry, sad photo albums, and (ostensibly) no job . . . then I lose my business edge.

CHAPTER 12

CHAZ-RONYM...

SEEING

EVERYTHING

GOING

AWAY

LATELY

MEGA
1988

February 9-11
Davenport, IA
Civic Center

CHAPTER 13

Presenter • Exhibitor • Booth B6

This Isn't Just Any Golf Shirt;
I Was Keynote Speaker at
This Conference In 2004

Conferences are, as we know, an amazing way to sell books, build platform, and make valuable business connections. They also, occasionally, serve other purposes.

For me, they're a great way to expand my wardrobe and continue building my brand. In my closet are no less than 138 unique conference golf shirts—procured from gift bags that I've collected during my tenure as a sought-after speaker on social media and marketing. As a result, it's been four years since I've purchased a new shirt.

Here's a random sample of the shirts I've collected:

- **CBA** (Christian Bookseller's Association), 2005.

- **Moody Pastor's Conference**, 2007.

- **Together for the Gospel**, 2008 / **Gospel Coalition**, 2008 (this was actually the same conference, due to a glitch on the GCO website and a printing error on the conference brochures)

- **IGNITE!** 2009. I couldn't, for the life of me, tell you what this was about. I do remember that the conference organizers declared bankruptcy on day four of the five-day conference.

- **Acquire the Fire**, 2010. This was either an evangelical youth retreat, or the annual meeting of the State Border Firework Merchant's Association.

- **PASSION!** 2004

- **CREATIVITY!** 2005

- **CULTURE!** 2006

- **CONFERENCE!** 2003

- **COMMUNITY!** 2007

- **Breathe**, 2012. This was either a small collective of West Michigan writers, or the American Association of Oxygen Tank Suppliers. (I was doing their social media for a while.)

In addition to the shirts, I've also amassed a collection of 176 faux-leather "portfolios." I have 1,200 free ink pens, and will (Lord willing) never have to purchase another pen in my life. As you can see, conferences can be extremely important. The **"Conferences are a great way to expand your wardrobe."** shirts aren't just shirts though—they are sartorial conversation-starters. I can't tell you how many times I've been out and about, at the mall, at the grocery store, or taking yet another lonely, soul-searching evening walk, when some-body has said, "Hey, weren't you the breakout speaker in Meeting Room C at the Ramada Inn's COM-MUNITY! conference in 2007?"

At which point I reply, "Why yes I was." Sometimes these conversations result in a new Twitter follower. In best cases, they result in someone buying me dinner. Only once have they resulted in a fist fight (long story).

CHAPTER 13
CHAZ-RONYM...

GETTING

ONLINE,

LEVERAGING

FORTUNE

MEGA
1998
February 3-11
Davenport, IA
Civic Center

CHAPTER 14

Presenter • Exhibitor • Booth B6

I Feel So [expletive] Alone:

Transcript of Inaugural Video Podcast
(working title, *Business and
All That Chazz*)

Hello, is this thing on? [indiscernible noises, including those of a thumb thumping the end of a microphone and also papers being shuffled] . . . I just got a new USB microphone for my laptop and . . . [garbled] . . .

Welcome to the inaugural podcast of "Business and All That Chazz," which is a clever play on the well-known phrase "All That Jazz," which was also the title of a Broadway musical. Think of this podcast . . . [cough, cough] . . . as the Broadway musical of business podcasts, meaning that it will have the same kind of entertainment value, minus the costumes, actors, stage lights, and music. Rather, it will be me here in my apartment speaking into a webcam and a USB microphone, talking about business and business issues.

I'll be joined sometimes by a man whom I'm quite certain is former Hollywood actor Steven Segal . . . Steven [off camera] . . . [A pause as Segal ostensibly walks through the room]

[expletive] [by Segal]

He'll be appearing periodically because we share the same living space, which I like to think of as an incubator for creative thought and business excellence. It's also where we keep our karate equipment and eat many of our meals . . .

[beeping of a microwave] [another expletive as Segal is burned by a hot bowl of Top Ramen]

I can't overstate the importance of podcasting. Podcasting, to the uninitiated, may seem like simply giving away product for free. It may seem like a semi-pointless expenditure of time and in some cases money. It may mean that you'll be at the mercy of your neighbor's unsecured wireless connection which has a way of giving out at critical moments of you—

[18 seconds of blank screen]

Sorry folks, I'm Chaz Marriot and this is "All That Chazz." Steven [off camera], can you please not walk in front of that window because it compromises the Internet connection. Thanks.

[sound of a garbled voice and a door closing]

You may think Mr. Segal's voice is garbled

because of this USB microphone, but it actually sounds that way in real life.

Anyway, podcasting is a great way to reach your constituents with a message that is a lot of work for you, but which they don't have to pay any-thing for. That's the beauty of podcasting (for them). The idea here is that if they get enough of your pro-duct for free in the form of 20-30 minute–but not longer—podcasts and videos, they will even-tually, magically, someday decide to start paying you for that product.

"Podcasting may seem like a semi-pointless expenditure of time and in some cases money."

If other companies applied this same logic—and I hope they do—then Nike would be giving away free basketball shoes and I wouldn't have to play my pickup game at the "Y" in this pair of dock shoes from the 1990s.

[pauses to show dock shoes]

[pause for what feels like several minutes but is really only, like, 90 seconds]

I can't believe I'm doing this. I can't believe I'm alone—completely alone—in a studio apartment speaking into a tiny, round dot on the top of my antiquated Toshiba laptop. I can't believe that anyone considers this "cutting edge" given the low-quality of this image and also given the way my chin looks from this angle.

[pauses to adjust angle]

Sigh.

I mean what I'm really trying to get at here . . . conceptually . . . is the idea of—and the irony in— the fact that although I've spent my life trying to build a quote/unquote platform, what I'm doing at this moment is being completely and utterly alone and speaking into a USB microphone in such a way as to suggest that I have "followers" **[makes air quotes]** and an "audience" **[ibid, re: the air quotes]** when in reality the likelihood of somebody downloading "All That Chazz" and actually listening to it and actually caring about it is about the same, probability-wise, as Mr. Segal inviting me to hang out with him at Eric Roberts's condo to celebrate Memorial Day.

Also, it's Memorial Day. And I don't have anything to do . . .

[pause for what sounds like sniffling]

The thing of it is, is that sometimes I have trouble even getting out of bed in the morning and, like, convincing myself that any of this is worthwhile. I mean if you think I actually care whether you quote/unquote grow your quote/unquote platform, then I've got a golf course to sell you on the outskirts of Lansing right near the Lansing/East Lansing border, adjacent to an electronic cigarette stand and a Sears.

Actually, I do have that. And I would really like to sell it. *Sigh.*

What is real is that I don't know who I am anymore. I mean . . . I know that I'm Chaz Marriot but did you know that that isn't even my real name? It isn't . . . but I'm not going to tell you my real name because that's a level of self-disclosure and, you know, intimacy, that I'm not so comfortable with yet. What I mean is that I don't know why I'm here. I don't know why any of us are here . . . I mean, there are just so many people. Do you ever wonder what they're all doing? Do you ever wonder, like, why they're here, per se? Do you ever wonder what gives them fulfillment? I bet it's not updating their Twitter feeds and Facebook statuses several times a day in such a way as to drive website traffic and throughput.

[sounds of cereal being eaten, off camera]

I'm eating cereal on my podcast. This is media. This is entertainment. At this moment you're listening to me eating cereal.

I'm so lonely. I miss my family so much. I've spent my entire life trying to be famous enough and impressive enough to them, so as to make them proud of me, but the irony of it all is that they just want me around or at least that's what they said via a handwritten letter I received at the dojo downstairs, which is where I receive my mail.

I'm so tired. I mean, not physically tired . . . but more like a psychic sort of spiritual sort of fatigue. Kind of. It's a pervasive kind of dark, settling fatigue that makes activities like taking out the garbage and binge-watching "Cheers" feel tiresome. I don't even want to check my social media anymore. I have sixteen blogs . . . sixteen.

[long pause]

I just want to go home . . . I want to never get online again. I want to never ascend a stage again only to hear the sort of polite, post-lunch applause that says (figuratively), "I'm just here for the grilled chicken and also because my company paid to send me here and this is better than sitting in the office, slowly having the life sucked out of me." I want to never wear a conference golf shirt again. I never want to hear the words "grip and grin." I never again want to tell anyone that their book idea has potential and they should consider getting it published and they should consider hiring me to do their publicity. I want to never again then hand that person a business card and then promise to catch up with them later, which I will do via telephone call exactly 36 hours later so that they feel quote/unquote valued and remembered but not quote/unquote pressured.

[sounds of mouse clicking—Marriot's eyes moving frantically around the screen]

Do you hear that sound? It's the sound of me shutting down my Twitter account. It's also the sound of me deleting blogs. It's the sound of the online entity known as Chaz Marriot disappearing. *Sigh.*

[the sounds of tears being wiped away]

Compose yourself, Marriot [to himself]. Come on, now.

[the sounds of a letter being opened, unfolded and, we can assume, read . . . the sounds of a bag being packed, meaning the rustling of nylon along with the rustling of cotton and pants-material]

[the sound of a door opening]

[Segal, from off camera] *Hey, a few of us are . . .* [garbled] *. . . getting together over at Eric Roberts's pool . . . wanna join us?*

[The sound of a computer being powered down and clicked shut]

CHAPTER 14
CHAZ-RONYM

PERIODICALLY

OVERWHELMING

DEVASTATION

MEGA
1998

February 9-11
Davenport, IA
Civic Center

APPENDICES

Presenter • Exhibitor • Booth B6

Appendix A: Graphing the Effectiveness of This Book vs. the Fact That All of the Content Will Be Obsolete By the Time You Finish Reading

Legally, I need to be up front and tell you that nearly all business book content is obsolete by the time it hits the shelves. That said, if you're an average-to-good reader, and only you truly know how good a reader you are, you can still get a lot out of *Mega*. The beauty of *Mega*: it's not just a business book, rather, it's a beautiful narrative unfolding on the backdrop of business. Which is to say that business is a part of it, yes, but what it really is, is an authentic look inside the heart and soul of a man, putting it on par with such books as *The Sun Also Rises*, *To Kill a Mockingbird*, and the great business book *Blue Like Jazz*.

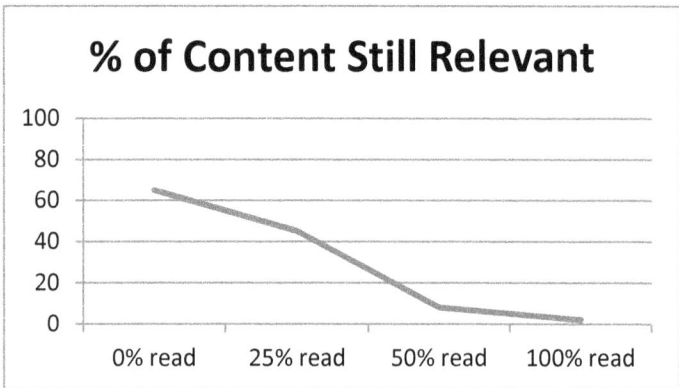

% of Content Still Relevant

100	
80	
60	
40	
20	
0	

0% read　25% read　50% read　100% read

Appendix B: How Many Times You Should Be Tweeting Per Day

200.

Appendix C:
Different Platforms (Plus Schematics)

When I tell people I'm writing a book about platform, sometimes they'll get very practical and ask what "type" of platform I'm referring to. After I tell them to loosen up and think out of the "box" (which in this case isn't a real box but is, in fact, a rhetorical device meaning a standardized way of thinking), I tell them that "platform," for our purposes, doesn't mean an elevated wooden thing on which you can place trinkets, trophies, books, or even in the case of outdoor platforms, a picnic table. Rather, a platform for our purposes means a group of people who will potentially buy your product and has nothing to do with surfaces on which to place things.

However, a good many people are interested in surfaces on which to place things, which is why I've included these handy schematics. Enjoy.

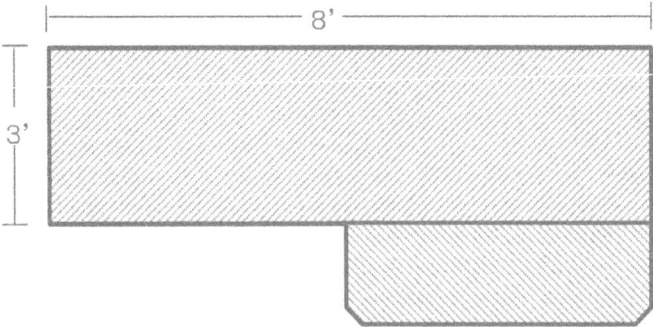

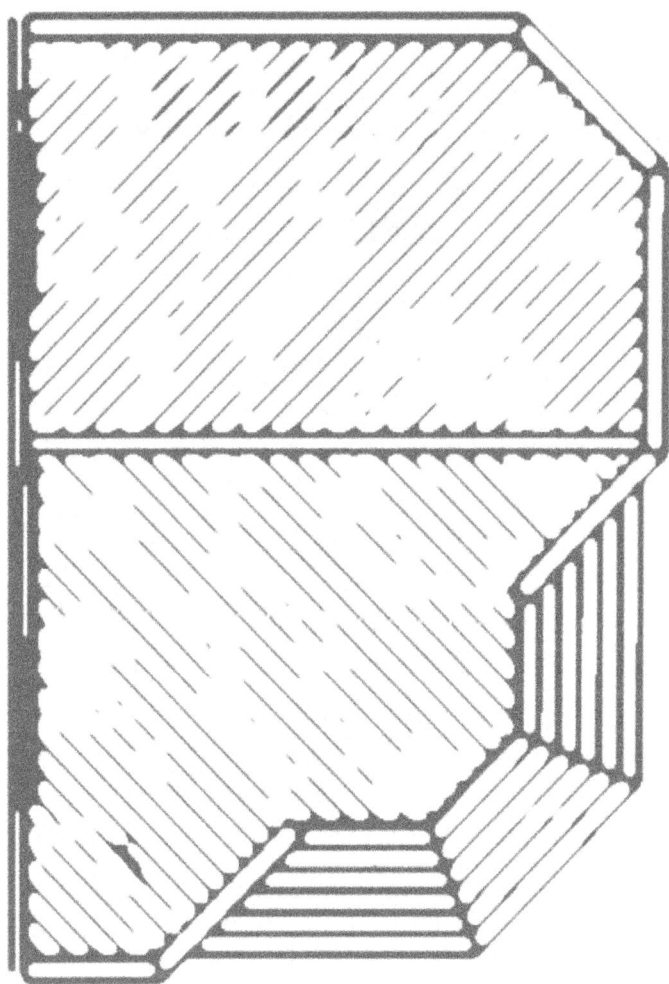

Appendix D: More Terminology

Best Practices: This is a purpose-driven seeker-sensitive term meaning that "I can steal and implement something you do and call it my own, provided it came from a seminar or webinar or series of emails entitled *Best Practices*."

Reframing: This is what you do when you've presented an idea that people don't like. In reframing, you basically give them the same idea, but just make it sound a little bit different so that they'll embrace it. If this sounds unethical, it isn't. Reframing is also what you sometimes do with old pictures.

Profilaction: Taking action to update your social media profiles 2-3 times per day, meaning updating your bio and changing pictures.

Core Competency: A term I invented to identify a few key things you do well. Also an ab-blasting class I take at Bally's Total Fitness in the Dadeland Strip Mall, on Tuesdays and Thursdays. (Note: If I enroll a friend I get a free t-shirt.)

Cannibalization: What happens when one online presence undermines the integrity of another, thus "cannibalizing" it. Also what happens in certain Central American villages where you crash your Cessna Citation on the way to the Super Bowl.

Career Suicide: What happens when you do something so stupid that it derails the remainder of your career. Also what happens when you wake up naked, in the fetal position, in Shaquille O'Neal's fountain at his retirement party.

De-Purpose: A kinder term for firing someone. Ex: "We're going to have to de-purpose you because of the career suicide you committed at the 2011 IGNITE! Conference."

Plates Spinning: A clever way to describe how many projects you have going at a particular time. Ex: "I have a lot of plates spinning right now." Also what happens when you date a particular kind of girl from Okemos, who likes to throw plates at your head when she gets angry.

Appendix E: Booking Chaz Marriot

Book Chaz for your next corporate outing, conference, wedding reception, graduation address, Rotary Club[22] meeting, or child's business-themed birthday party! Simply send an email to **bookchaz@gutcheckpress.com** with the name of the event in the subject line and answers to the following questions:

1. Will you be providing a ride to/from the airport?

2. Will there be bottles of water provided?

A representative of Chaz Marriot, or from one of Chaz Marriot's subcorporations will be in touch with you within 6-8 weeks. Or maybe longer. Or immediately if the Internet is working in the apartment.

---

[22] The Rotary Club of America does not acknowledge or approve this mention.

Appendix F: Conference-Worn Items

Business personality Chaz Marriot is selling, for a limited time on eBay (which is a successful online auction website) a selection of conference-worn apparel, including:

- Chaz's name badge from PASSION! 2004 (starting at $75)

- Chaz's breakout-session worn khaki pants from CREATIVITY! 2005 (starting at $150)

- Chaz's keynote-worn golf shirt from CULTURE! 2006 ($150 buy it now)

- Chaz's attendee bracelet from BUZZWORD! 2007 ($25)

- Chaz's cease and desist letter from the legal team representing Shaquille O'Neal ($15)

- Chaz's gas-station receipt from May 2014 ($4)

Appendix G: Excerpt of Chaz Marriot's Screenplay, Working Title: *Hard to Kill*

                                    CUT TO:
INT: STUDIO APARTMENT, DAY

Ruggedly handsome business executive and spy
SHANE HYATT reclines on a high-end leather
sofa, eating an expensive cut of steak and
watching a larger-than-average flat screen
television when in bursts IVAN ALTROGGE, a
part-time musician and underground Latvian
arms dealer. In one deft movement, Hyatt
leaps from the sofa, glass of port still in
hand, and puts Altrogge in an arm-bar, at
which point he begins bantering with him
cleverly in the way that awesome spies
always banter cleverly with people they
might be about to kill.

                    SHANE HYATT
          Your platform will never be as
          big as mine!

                    IVAN ALTROGGE
          Is that a veiled reference to
          something?

                    SHANE HYATT
          Come again?

                    IVAN ALTROGGE
          You're such a hack, Hyatt. I
          couldn't help but notice how you
          left a magazine full of hollow-
          point 9MM bullets behind in your
          booth at the upscale Italian
          eatery, Cuginos.

                    SHANE HYATT
You think you're so clever Altrogge
(wrenches arm-bar tighter). I
always do that. So much so that the
waitresses always just grab them
for me and leave them in a box in
the back. Also, those bullets are
fake.

                   IVAN ALTROGGE
What? Who carries fake bullets?

                    SHANE HYATT
What? (wrenches arm bar tighter
still . . . drops glass of port)

                   IVAN ALTROGGE
If you're going to kill me, Hyatt,
just do it now. Get it over with.

                    SHANE HYATT
I'm not going to do that because of
the begrudging respect I have for
you, even though I hate you. I'm
going to stoop down to pick up my
glass of port, at which point
you'll flee from the apartment,
stopping only to empty a couple of
rounds into the plaster drywall
behind the sofa, which will cause
the plaster to crack and fly off
dramatically but nobody will be
hurt.

                   IVAN ALTROGGE
That's the dynamic of the group.

NOTE: Any Hollywood executives reading "MEGA" who would like
to option "Hard to Kill," please email scripts@chazmarriot.com

Painfully Over-the-top-Disclaimer

This book is a business / networking / platform book but it's also a satire. Okay, it's mostly a satire. Okay, it's all a satire.

That being said, the people in it aren't real, even if we sometimes use their real names. For example, nobody whose name we mention in conjunction with having been in Chaz Marriot's apartment has actually been in Chaz Marriot's apartment because Chaz Marriot's apartment doesn't exist. Disclaimer to the disclaimer: You have probably already inferred this from what I just wrote, but if not, Chaz Marriot also doesn't exist.

Because of that, he / Chaz never actually roomed with Steven Seagal (yes, we know it's spelled "Seagal") who, even though I write funnily about him in this book, we (Gut Check, collectively) actually think is pretty awesome because we sort of benefitted from having watched "Hard to Kill" and "Marked for Death" and [other title having to do with killing or death] when we were teenagers.

Also: We think John Schlitt and Petra are pretty much great too. Ditto for LeCrae - the French pastry chef and the rapper.

Even though Chaz Marriot isn't real, per se, there are real people who are really writing this kind of book (about social media, about getting noticed, about "platform", about that being more important than content, about that being the most important thing) except that they're not doing it as a joke. And that's the part we think is funny.

So, as is the case with all Gut Check Press titles, we invite you to join us in thinking this is funny. Except that if you're going to get all thin and serious about it and get offended by it, we un-invite you.

Sincerely,
The Gut Check Press Executive Team
Gut Check Press Headquarters
New York, New York
(meaning, Altoona, PA)
(meaning, actually, Lansing, Michigan)

About the Author

Chaz Marriot is the author of several books on the topics of success and leadership and winning. If Chaz were an animal he'd be a lion because lions are the king of the jungle. And also because of Chaz's hair. He describes himself as "The William Wallace of Enthusiasm" meaning that he's metaphorically-speaking ready to charge down a hill and cut you in half with his enthusiasm. Chaz's passions are team-building, visioning, creative synergy, focus grouping, meetings, and cheesesteak sandwiches. Chaz once bench-pressed 405 pounds.

He further describes himself as the "Vince Lombardi of Team Building" because even though everyone hated Vince Lombardi, he was still very successful. Chaz also enjoys making his own soda. This is his fourteenth book.

More Books from

Gut Check Press™

The Christian Gentleman's
Smoking Companion

Younger, Restlesser,
Reformeder

Kinda Christianity

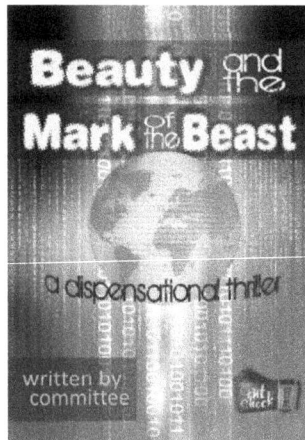

Beauty and the Mark
of the Beast

www.gutcheckpress.com

42 Months Dry:
A Tale of Gods and Gunplay

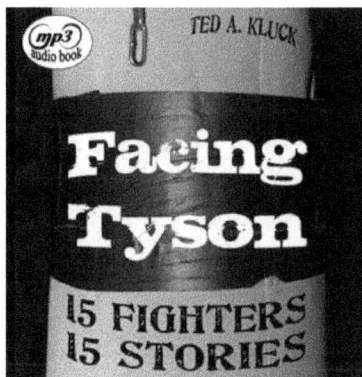

Facing Tyson:
15 Fighters, 15 Stories
Audio Book

Saucy Broad:
A Culinary Manifesto of Hope

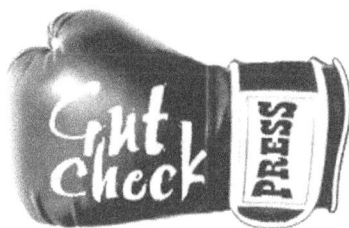

Making Your
Publishing
Company Feel
Small and Weak
Since 2010